Breaking Loose Now

Freedom From Within

Sofia Edlund

Introduction

This book is conceived with the aim to help you find freedom from within. With so many stressors and people saying you will never amount to much, it is easy to slip in to a depressive state and simply give up hope of ever being free from the chains that bind you. Finding freedom is so much more than you think. It does not matter what people think of you. You don't need anybody's approval before reaching for the skies and breaking loose from all that has been holding you back. Emotional intimidation, abandonment, addiction and inhibitions are some of the challenges we all have to face sometime in our lives. It is our ability to rise above the blues that will set us on the sure path to freedom.

Most of the problems we encounter in life have to do with the need to constantly improve ourselves, correct our mistakes, make up for past mistakes, in-fighting within our subconscious, suppression of negative feelings, censoring the way we think and so on. If we keep trying to make up for a tirade of several helpless situations and sometimes play the blame game with our subconscious, it may lead to self-denial and self- justification. The basic requirement for happiness is to completely accept ourselves the way we are. Oh, how easy it will be to avoid mental health problems with an inward and outward acceptance of ourselves that is absolute and unconditional.

Perhaps, I will draw you out to accept 2 important facts about yourself. It will give a basis from which to start the self-healing processes. The first is that the past is exactly what it is – the past. It is best to allow it to remain where it is and realize you have no power to rewind the hands of time. Learn to live with it and accept it with no feelings of regret. The second fact is along similar lines as the first. It is this; only your actions can harm people. Your thoughts, emotions and feelings will never cause harm to others. Choose to accept them and only then will you be able to have more control over your actions.

Never be at the receiving end of your criticisms. Continually flog yourself and you may never summon up the courage to rise while you are down. Love yourself unconditionally. This is the only way you will be able to break free from the shackles of self-criticism and depression. Nobody can make you feel bad unless you give them the permission to do so. Say to yourself today, "It all begins with me. Why crawl when I can soar?" Flying is all about freedom. No one can fly while being held down in chains. In the same way, why fight something you know you cannot change? You are the only one holding yourself down. Do you know it is so easy for you to be dominated and controlled by others if you are divided within yourself? A house divided cannot stand. The common solution is to allow the divided parts to merge into one indivisible whole.

Here is a simple exercise to help you understand the concept of division and unity. When pressure is applied to a single broomstick, it is easy for it to break into several pieces depending on what points the pressure is applied. Imagine when single broom sticks are brought together to make a bunch. A bunch of broom consists of several hundreds and thousands of individual sticks. No amount of pressure applied to a bunch of brooms will make it break. Remember that individually these broom sticks can be broken with a flick of the finger but when these tiny single strands are brought together, they become formidable. Try as much as you might to break them, a bunch of broom remains firm and will hold on to one another steadfastly.

Each part of yourself that you battle with is like a single strand of broom that you pick with your fingers and break to pieces. Only continuous and unconditional acceptance will bring these single parts of yourself together to form one formidable and unshakable broom. This is something worth thinking about.

There is a constant battle between good and evil; the battle to do that which we perceive to be good and shun that which the society abhors. This battle can sometimes tear us apart. Our perception of good and evil differs and but one thing stands out. It is that the concept of good is that which promotes our wellbeing and by extension the society in which we find ourselves. The feeling that something is evil generally means that which affects our perception of good negatively. There may be truth in the saying that all we perceive as evil are rather shadows of the real thing. Consider the selfish acts being carried out every day by people who should otherwise know better and you will get a dim idea of how evil negatively affects the society.

Perhaps it will be too harsh to term as evil an act of selfishness no matter how minor (an evil). But when we consider the fact that selfishness not only interferes with the free flow of information but it also subjugates and imposes its will on the susceptible, making you a slave to the whims and caprices of people whose intensions are less than honorable, then we will be begin to see the merits of considering selfishness as an evil. Granted, minor acts of selfishness like taking monopoly of the TV remote is nowhere near being evil. For an act to be actively evil, it must cause significant harm and suffering to the oppressed. Evil is essentially the imposition of will. Anything that will take away the life, dignity, property and humanity of someone (away from him) against his wish (is essentially evil). Invariably, these behaviors affect the health of the society. There is no other way to explain acts sanctioned by societies in which cruelty is exalted other than evil. Consider the menace of Boko Haram, the Holocaust, terrorism and you will begin to glimpse into the heart of societal evil. These instances are bad because it seeks to control by breeding fear.

There are instances when evil may be considered necessary. In this case, the phrase "necessary evil" comes into focus. When we impose our will on someone else in other to prevent that person from perpetuating greater evil and destruction, then we would have used a necessary evil to put a stop to a situation. The truth of the matter is that evil can never be used to stop evil. What we can only achieve is a short term solution. In the long run we will only have encouraged more evil to be done. Healing from within is the only sure way that society and individuals can be free from the shackles of evil.

There is the inherent feeling in man to dominate and impose on others. More often than not, this is destructive and will lead to contempt; contempt for ourselves and contempt for the wish of others. Hostile behavior is an indication of contempt of self. When you threaten and abuse a child or woman, you are only feeling contempt for the inner child in you and the feminine side that has been abandoned respectively. You may not want to accept that there is an inner child somewhere in you that is yearning to be loved and cared for.

Open acceptance of self leads to a lack of hostility. We may feel troubled or even sad about the hostility of others and to a large extent oppose it but we will not go out of our way to experience hostility. In a bid to protect our family from a deranged person, we may kick and lash out and even shoot the deranged if the life of our family is at stake. But that does not mean we feel hostile to the threat. In our mind's eye we see that this deranged person is only acting as his character proposes. Thus, we see that if we do not have the same qualities which predispose the deranged to be hostile, there is no need to be hostile. What we do is only to protect our turf. What we can surmise here is that our state of inner dividedness is the origination of evil and not necessarily the expression of our primary inclination or nature.

Religion would have us believe that evil is another name for selfishness and this is something to be ashamed of. However, modern philosophers are quick to dispute this idea with the notion that selfishness is something that is inbuilt in us. According to this school of thought, selfishness is essential to the survival of species on earth.

The religious and philosophic schools are thought have got it all wrong. Selfishness does not arise from the need to propagate the human genes. Neither does it have anything to do with survival of species. What we have is a society that is so sick that it is at pains. Selfishness is not genetic. It stems from a mind and body that is so sick that it cares for nothing else other than self. When a person feels pain – either physical or emotional – it is difficult for the person to concentrate on something else other than the pain. Give me a happy and healthy person and I will give you someone who will forget self and concentrate on the needs of others.

Selfishness from the perspective of the sufferer is only wrong if s/he doesn't know how to help her/himself. It is quite understandable to concentrate on ourselves when sick so as to find ways of curing our sickness. When no cure is in the horizon, we may seek to distract ourselves and derive short term relief and pleasure in other to mask our state. But the question arises as to what defines a state of health. A healthy person will only seek to do what s/he will without being compelled to submit to a situation or ideal. This person is healthy if her/his desire to do whatever s/he will does not carry with it any form of destructive tendencies and does not leave sorrow and regret in its wake. If there is no way for a person to do this, s/he is invariably sick.

The only cure that I know for destructive tendencies is by continuous and unconditional acceptance of self. This is the only known cure for the disease of selfishness. A person divided from within needs to accept all facets of her/his personality. Only then can they be on the path to true healing that begins from within.

You Are Worth So Much More

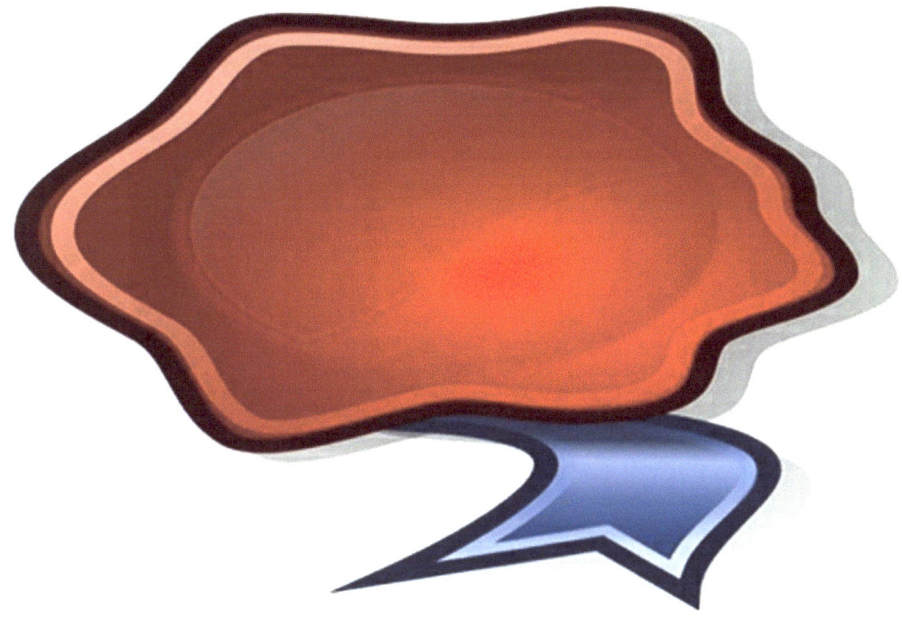

Psychology teaches us that we are all habitual self-evaluators. How then do we judge our self-worth? Is it by how others perceive us? Does it have anything to do with our ego and self-image? It is never an easy thing to make the best of our culturally conditioned self-evaluation. To put away our judgmental self-evaluation, we need to practice self-acceptance. You will need to rehearse the belief of self-acceptance within yourself and truly earn it.

Rehearse to yourself this belief *"I am worthwhile because I exist, I am I, and I am alive."* Adopt this new way of thinking as a mantra and create a healthy transformation within yourself.

The sum total of the belief in self-assurance is that there are no evil people, just evil behaviors. Society reserves the right to hold us responsible for this thought. Your belief in your own self-worth is a more realistic and practical way of liberating yourself and embracing self-acceptance. Embrace this belief with all your heart and you will be strengthened and armed with the tool to extinguish evil behaviors that lurks just beneath the surface. Let me ask you thought provoking questions. Are you prepared to accept yourself unconditionally and unreservedly just the way you are? Do you believe that you are you, you are alive and you exist? Do you believe that this system would add value to your life? Answer positively to these questions and you are ready to come alive and realize you are worth so much more.

You have a choice to either be a habitual self-evaluator or accept yourself the way you are. You can choose to go through life for all the wrong reasons and end up back in square one. But you can also choose to accept unreservedly that you are a worthwhile venture. This will enable you strive to go through life for all the right reasons. The goal is to remember that you are worth so much more!

Much More Than Just a John/Jane Doe

A John/Jane Doe is that unidentifiable individual in the morgue. No one knows how s/he ended up dead. No one can say for sure who he is or from whence he came. He is that corpse with no identity with no-one to claim the remains. A John/Jane Doe can stay in the morgue for as long as possible until someone finally comes along to identify her/him. Sometimes, a John/Jane Doe will end up being buried in an unmarked grave with no-one to shed tears, no-one to give eulogies and no-one to reflect on the life s/he has lived.

Your life is so much remarkable than a John/Jane Doe. How you decide your life to play out is entirely up to you. There are many shades of truth just as there are many shades of reality. The reality that works is one in which you visualize yourself standing head and shoulders above the crowd. Picture yourself as a valuable member of a group. See yourself as someone with value that is priced above rubies. It may be said that a lack of self-worth relegates us to the background. Add in a touch of regret and blend it in with self-hate, and you will see how easy it is to slip into depression and become just another John/Jane Doe.

You are so much more than a John/Jane Doe. Your life has meaning; give it the direction it needs. The world cannot dictate what shape your life takes but you have the power to decide what colour you want your life to be. Realize that you have it in you to be so much more than you are at present. You may not brave enough to do what has to be done but you need to reach inside and find bravery. The world is a perception of how you want it to be. Choose to be positive and reach for the inner child in you that is happy and brave. Your obstacles will evaporate as you realize that you so much more than just a John/Jane Doe.

Embrace Your Imperfection; It's Part of Who You Are

It is impossible to find that person who is perfect in every sense of the word. This is a fact that most people accept.

Yet, there is always a part of us that strives towards perfection. A part that uses perfection as a yard stick to measure how well we have done in life. Perfection is nothing more than an illusion; the more we chase it the further it escapes us.

The universe as we know it is made up of several imperfect systems that have come together to provide a rhythm. Energy and matter is always in a state of entropy; bouncing off one another yet creating coordination that is difficult to understand. Surprisingly, this constant state of entropy in the system is what works for us. Complex matter is what keeps the system alive and well.

Life itself came about as a result of evolution. Evolution is the outcome of mutations that are random and disorganized. Were life to be perfect, evolution and mutations would have been series of organized events that works in tandem with one another. Instead what we have is a life force that came about from random unplanned events. Yet out of that imperfection came something beautiful and worthy. All the imperfection brought us a new branch on the tree of life. We got it all wrong when we forgot that we came out of imperfection and instead expect ourselves to be perfect in every sense of the word. That was when our troubles started. We looked down on our mistakes and became intolerant of our weaknesses. The imperfection that brought us where we are now became a vice that must be eradicated at all cost.

To achieve a new state of awareness, we must embrace our imperfections. They are an intrinsic art of who we are. They are what make us unique. Perfection, as elusive as it is is only a sterile existence. Embrace your imperfections and seek to make the best out of your life.

What has Religion got to do with it?

It is the nature of man to personalize the impersonal. As such we would often refer to earth's ecosystem as the Mother Nature. This is the same with our concept of religion. Each religion has a deity it pays allegiance to and because of this we have the concept of a God or gods;

depending on how we want to look at it. Just as Mother Nature, which we cannot put a face to; the idea of God or gods does not mean they really exist. Giving a deity human face is mankind's way of comforting himself.

The reality is that the universe is an observable force which operates on the laws of evolution, all functioning to create harmony. How then can religion conceive the idea of a deity which cannot be seen and which seeks to subjugate us all under its influence and control? Perhaps, the only plausible explanation is man's need for perfection. This perfection is held up as the ultimate ideals in order to keep us in line because of our neurotic nature.

Religion brought with it many intricacies which humans were quick to accept because by the time religion was foist upon us, we were already neurotic. Civilization, a form of repression did not help matters as it has been going on for a long time and it is only proper that the ideals of religion will be quickly clung onto. The leaders of the society are made up of the most neurotic members who seek to control the lesser neurotic. Our neurosis as a society stems from our fear of the abandoned part of our base nature. When these fears go unchecked, it results in the massive control of those who express these fears. When the society felled into a state of neurosis, there is the need by the more neurotic in the society to control and impose on their will on others less neurotic. For some reason, most deities are projected as males because it is the males in our society that are more prone to neurosis. Inevitably, the society became patriarchal and hence the idea of a most gods as Men; albeit angry male gods with the propensity to dispense justice. Thus, we see that the projection of most gods as males is simply a result of the manifestation of our self-image.

Religion became an active means through which a society already in neurosis is kept in order. It is generally accepted that the structure which we have built for ourselves is what works. This structure has kept us inline and allowed us develop and advance. The main drawback to this false sense of security which the society has created is that it failed to pinpoint what was at the root of the sickness into which the society has been plunged; this sickness being neurosis. It is not difficult to see that a major lack of self-acceptance is at the root of the problem. For this reason, mankind will always hold up the ideal of perfection as a yardstick from which we judge ourselves.

No Negotiations; Accept Yourself for Who You Are

Accepting yourself for who you truly are requires that you embrace all aspects of your personality and be at peace with them. In a way, I'd say that radical self-acceptance will bring together all parts of you that are damaged, beautiful, powerful, remorseful and divine. These parts must join together to form one great whole. Your perception of self must be not be through blurred lens but it must be seen with clean, clear, accurate lens. Accepting yourself for who you truly are requires that you address 5 key components of self. These are the mental, spiritual, physical, emotional and sexual. I will briefly discuss each of these points.

Physical acceptance of self: your body is an object of love and should be seen from this perspective. Notice all the amazing qualities and things your body can do. Is there a part that is easily neglected? This is the part to pay most attention to. Your organs exist to serve you; you should be grateful for that. Is there a part of your body you would wish to be different? Look at this body part with a sense of compassion. Visualize this part of your body changing for good. Embrace the imperfection of your body if it is not something you can change and send it abundant love.

Acceptance of mind: the mind is a cloud filled with infinite possibilities. Just as it is easy to visualize thoughtful goals with the mind, it is also possible to allow the mind be filled with goal derailing thoughts because of our fears. Accept your mental self the way it is. This means becoming aware of all the spectrums of your mind. Get acquainted with your fears and positive energies. Embrace it as part of who you are. When you create this awareness, you can choose to fill your mind with positive possibilities while eliminating the negatives.

Emotional acceptance of self: our emotions are tied to our experiences. Emotional being is linked to joy, anger, shame, sadness etc. Our emotions lead us to appreciate the opposites that constantly battle for attention within us. We cannot experience true happiness if we have not known pain. There is never full comprehension of compassion without having known shame. These opposites in our emotions complement each other. Do not work towards hiding or ridding yourself of shame. Accept it and feel it. Focus on your wounded parts and pay close attention to it. Only this way can you reduce the possibility that these parts will take you by surprise and make you feel bad. This is how you work to reduce the intensity of the pain you feel.

Spiritual acceptance of self: sometimes religion would have us believe that God is outside of ourselves. This is far from the truth. God is not something abstract that resides in an abode above the skies. God is within you. All that is good and divine is inside of you waiting to be recognized. Many times we forget that we are gods in our own right. We believe bad things about ourselves because we think we can never move past our mistakes or because the society dictates how we are supposed to see ourselves. When you accept your spirit, you are accepting that inside of you there is something wonderful and divine.

Sexual acceptance of self: accepting your sexuality is not just about your sexual orientation. It involves becoming intimate with yourself sexually. Many a time, victims of abuse tend to overplay or underplay their sexuality. This is neither gratifying nor loving. What is happening is that we are allowing ourselves to be stereotyped by the society in which we find ourselves. To love and embrace our sexuality, we must see it as the gateway to our divine energy. We must therefore see our sexuality as possessing integrity. Radically accept yourself the way you are and view it from a holistic point of view. Love of self, lack of judgment and show of compassion for ourselves will lead to sexual acceptance.

Defence Mechanism: Shield Protection

Armouring is a term used to define protection; physical and emotional protection. We may describe this type of defense mechanism as shield protection. Shield protection takes care of our body and character. In body shield protection, we are looking at a situation where the physical becomes a store house of our repressed emotions. A typical example of the body shield protection can be seen from the body language. It is not what is said or implied but what the body projects without speaking. A release is often experienced when the unspoken emotions being manifested in the body is dealt with. For example, a body massage can release pent up emotions of anger, tears and sadness and bring about pleasurable experiences.

In character shied protection, we see a system where our way of reasoning has become inflexible and defensive. This is more often than not caused by habit and stereotyping. This is in sharp contrast to the mind's original way of being open and taking a spontaneous burst at life.

The human shield usually goes up in response to external and internal aggression and dangers. This reaction becomes chronic as a defensive mechanism. Shied protection will go up some notches in unpleasant situations but when the condition becomes pleasant enough, it will go down many notches. We can begin to draw a difference between the neurotic and healthy shield protection depending upon the rate at which our defensive mechanisms are drawn up.

How it all began: a History of Neurosis

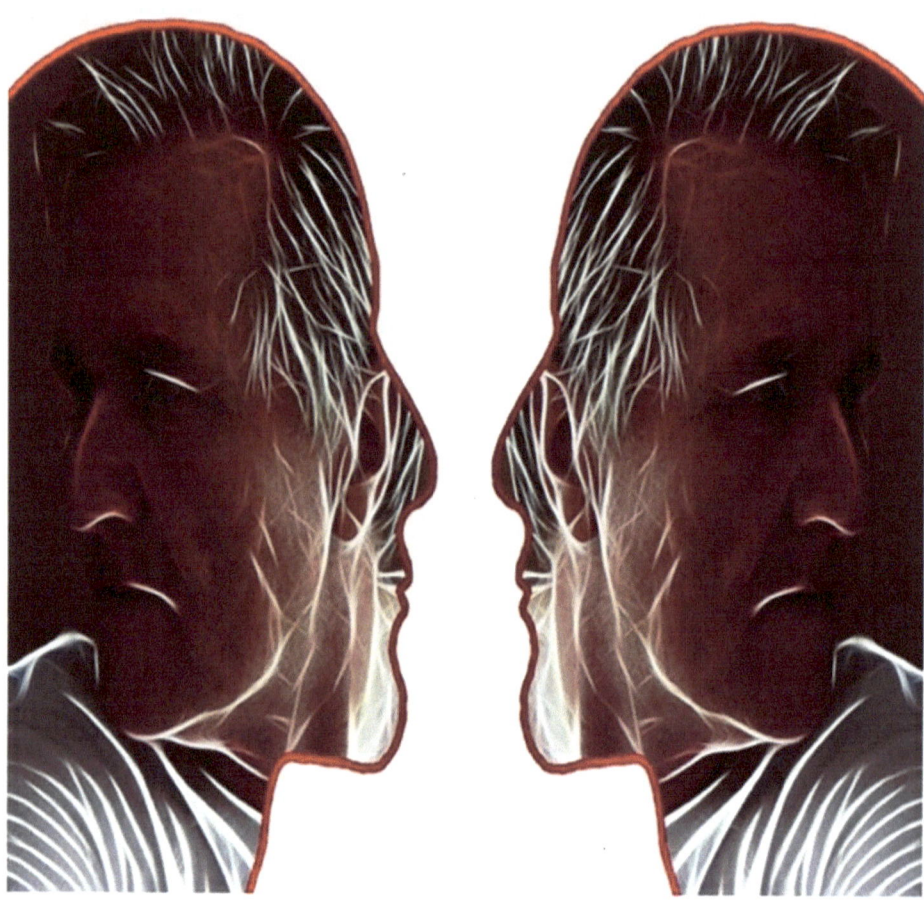

Human beings grow up needing something. It is not surprising that many people pass through life without their needs being met. The basic needs of humans are not excessive in any way. There is the need to be loved, to be held, to be fed, to grow, to develop at own pace, to be warm and dry as well as to be caressed. When a baby is born, these needs are at the forefront of its reality. This baby may not be aware that it needs these basics to survive. But when these needs go without being met, neurosis slowly creeps in. neurosis happens when a child's needs are not being met.

A baby will do all within his power to have his need met. When a baby cries, kicks and thrash about, it is a sign of the need to be fed, held or changed. He is reacting the only way he knows how for his needs to be met. He will continue to suffer until he gets the attention of his parents and his needs satisfied or he will learn to shut off his needs and bear his lot. How does a baby separate his senses from his consciousness so as to shut off excessive pain? This happens because the baby realizes that he cannot get this needs fulfilled all by itself. A baby cannot not fed itself or change his own diapers. As this realization sets in, the baby will instinctively know to separate his needs from himself. This is when the split occurs. This is a form of self-protection in order to shut off excessive pain.

When a split happens, it does not mean that the need suddenly disappears. This is not the case at all as the need will likely occur throughout life. What the individual does is to channel the pain and suppress it subconsciously. An alternative would be to seek substitute gratification methods. If only symbolically, the individual will strive to satisfy his needs and may compel others to listen and subject them to his will.

Needs that are not being met so much that they become painful will be relegated to the subconscious where they are easy to control. It is no wonder that suppressed feelings may be relieved by simple acts such as urination only to be replaced later by sex. A baby will learn to change his unfulfilled needs to symbolic ones. When he grows into adulthood, he may not have the urge to suck from the breasts of his mother because that need has been replaced by something as symbolic as smoking. This is where the root of neurosis lies; to replace the actual need by symbolic substitutes. Neurosis is caused by a need that is too painful to withstand such that the body shuts down in the bid to survive.

A real need is something that springs forth naturally. If a baby is not weaned too early, or forced to walk too early or even forced to feed himself too soon, his body's neurological apparatus will not be fully developed and such a child will be termed healthy. Neurosis originates from the non-satisfaction of natural needs which leads to unnatural or symbolic needs. A child may grow up craving to be praised because he is not loved enough by his parents. He may be made to feel that nothing he ever does is good enough to deserve praise. On the other hand, the suppression of verbal expression in childhood may lead to denial. Such denial may cause the child to feel the need to be a chatterbox.

A child that is well be loved is one whose natural needs are being met. When this child is hurt, that hurt is easily taken away by love. This child will not feel the need for praise because he is not being relegated to the background. This child will feel and know that he has value in himself because of what he is and not because of his parents expectations and what he does to satisfy them. A child that has known love all his life will never grow up to be someone with an unnatural and insatiable craving for sex. His needs have been met by being constantly held and caressed by his parents. This child will not feel the need to use sex to gratify his need for his parents touch and caresses. The need to be loved, held and caressed is something that comes from within; these are the real needs. Now compare this with a child who is unloved and is hurt because his needs are not being met. This can lead to undesirable consequences. Just as a healthy body needs sufficient stimulation to develop and grow, mental stimulation is necessary for the development of a healthy mind and soul. Neurosis is only the pathology of feeling because the body and mind is in a constant state of tension being disconnected from consciousness.

The first time a child shuts down his feeling is the start of the neurotic process but it is not when neurosis begins. The shutdown is done in stages. There will come a time when there will be a major emotional trigger that will turn the child off making him more unreal. This turning point is when we say that neurosis has fully arrived. The child will from this moment onwards experience something like a personality split in which he will switch between his real and unreal self. The real self stems from the original needs and feelings of the child but the unreal self tries to cover up the real self and make up for it in several ways. The unreal is a façade by the neurotic. A child who has been harassed and humiliated by his parents will grow up to become a parent who demands absolute and unflinching respect from his children. Children who do not challenge or sass him will do just fine. Another instance is a parent who is babyish and would want to remain a baby for too long. Such a parent may demand and do all in his power to make his children grow up too fast. He will pitch them into adulthood far before they are ready; all these so he can continue to be cared for as the baby he craves to be.

The unreal needs creep onto a child most unexpectedly. He is not always prepared and may not know how on earth it happened. The child is born to feel that his parents' needs are his command. He is pushed to smile even when he is feeling otherwise, get straight A's in school, be quiet and undemanding, be athletic, say all the right things, be helpful etc. It does not help that the demands become intense as he gets older. What this means is this child is never allowed to be himself. He is never allowed to pursue his dreams. His needs are repressed and denied by his consciousness. What his parents are invariably telling his consciousness is that he cannot do what he wants and expects to be loved by them. The pain begins because this child is not allowed fulfillment. The general feeling is: I am not loved and cannot be loved when I am my real self.

With each suppressant need, the child becomes more neurotic. With each passing assault on the real self, there is a crushing weight on the child. Until such a moment when all the depravations, humiliations, negation and traumatic experiences accumulate to create the feeling that he can never be loved; not while he is his real self.

This leads to the activation of a self-defense mechanism which I referred to as 'shield protection'. There is a split in feeling as the child gradually slides into neurosis. The child will act in the way and manner his parents expect him to even when they are not there until this behavior becomes instinctive and automatic. This split becomes a defensive mechanism through which the child protects his sanity and evades reality.

In being neurotic, an individual becomes something that he is not. He holds on to a fragment of his imagination that does not exist. Where there is love, neurosis would not be in existence because love involves allowing someone to be himself. It doesn't really take a traumatic experience for neurosis to begin. All it takes is an act that says to an individual that his emotions and feelings don't matter. It may take the form of something as simple as asking a child to always say "please" and "Thank you" at the end of every sentence. It may be not permitting anger from your child, or even forcing him to recite poems in front of an audience. All it takes is a spark of action that says "Be what I want you to be or else no love for you from me." Soon this becomes a ritual which the child must perform to gain approval.

The child must deal with the hopelessness of his situation sometime and this leads to a split. Realizing that he may never probably be loved and his needs may never be filled no matter what he does must be denied by all means if he is to cope with the reality of his situation. The only means available to him is to defend himself from harm is by substituting his needs for another, which is neurotic. A typical example that easily comes to mind is that of the child that is constantly being put down by his parents. To cover up for his needs, this child may chatter endlessly in the classroom so much so that his teacher may be forced to put a harsh stop to it. Again, this child may brag endlessly the least opportunity he gets in the schoolyard. This may alienate him from other children. At a later stage in his life, he will likely have other substitute needs such as demanding for the best table in the house. To the casual onlooker, he will appear controlling and loud.

Everyone is born with some real biological needs which cannot be met by the parents for some reasons. It is possible that parents do not really recognize that their child is needy and as such will ignore him. It is equally possible that some parents do not want make mistakes in child rearing and as such will follow methods prescribed by some authority figure and will attend to the child methodically and impersonally. It is possible that most neurosis did not begin because of the parents' methodical approach to child rearing. The most plausible idea is that parents in themselves while struggling with their childish nature and cravings are simply too busy to attend to the needs of the child.

A mother may simply get pregnant just because of her need to be pampered and babied. This is at the root of her pregnancy not because she came prepared for the process of child rearing. What she wants is to be the center of attention. As long as she gets the attention she craves, she will be happy - so to say. After giving birth depression naturally sets in because pregnancy has served her needs for a short while and she has suddenly realized it is her turn to baby someone else. Her needs have nothing to do with taking care of another human being and neither does she have the tools for such a responsibility. What follows is a period of suffering for the child for even daring to inconvenience the mother and deprive her of the time she could use in making people care for her. Not being fed very often, the breast milk will dry up leaving the baby with early deprivations which he will have to cope with later in life. There is an endless vicious cycle as parents' continue to visit on the child needless suffering caused by their own needy state.

When a child attempts to please his parents, it is called the struggle. The struggle starts first and foremost with the parents and in later life will be transferred to the world at large. This deprived individual will carry his needs wherever he goes and act out his need. He will seek symbolic parents or substitutes. Much later in life, he may make his children and everyone else in his life to play parental roles to him so that his needs will be met. If a parent as a child was suppressed verbally as a child, he may invariably force his children to listen to his tirade all day long. The children are in turn being forced to play the role of listeners and will also force their children into this same role so as to meet their needs of being listened to. And so the cycle continues.

There is a change in the focal point of the struggle from the real to the neurotic; because basic needs are not met and therefore there will be a rise in mental need. Mental needs are purely psychological which in turn is neurotic. Mental needs serve no real purpose for an individual. For example, the man who requires the best seat in the house is only doing so because of his need to feel important; probably because he has been deprived of love as a child and his real needs were suppressed. He may have the need to be recognized in any event or place – which is only symbolic of course – which means he is trying to substitute for the real needs of being recognized by his parents and not relegated to the background. If this man had received all the love and attention he could get, there would have been no need for the symbolic need to feel important. The neurotic will only put new labels to unconscious needs and pursue them relentlessly believing them to be the thing that really matters.

Struggle keeps an individual from acknowledging his helpless situation. This individual will have to work harder than others to achieve the best. All this is done in the hopes that he will be loved for his many efforts. He is not quite being himself anymore and soon he will believe this struggle to be the real thing. The need to see your name in the limelight; the need to shine and be appreciated by all and sundry is a sign that individual recognition was missing. It becomes a struggle to please the larger audience. Soon that act is no longer voluntary; it becomes automatic and unconscious. This is what neurosis is all about.

Drawing from Our Personal Experiences

Without further ado, we can draw from our early personal experiences to help us understand the process we have described previously. Our early experiences are a replicate of the history of our species, the Homo sapiens. Right from the moment we graced this world, we are filled with abundant love that is unconditional even in our needy nature. The unconditional loving nature of the baby we were born needs to be understood implicitly.

Love as seen from the eyes of a baby is neither compassion nor adoration. It is a form of communication that has nothing to do with our collective egos. This kind of love is often seen when we are really interested in a person and not somewhere else in our heads. Love changes us because we are in tune with the person with whom we love. The opposite of this all accepting love is being stereotypical, rigid and guarded. The ego is something that is insecure and will seek to protect itself through acts of self-justification and repression. Conversely, if we can sit down with someone and not feel the need to be guarded but instead really open up and engage in spontaneous communication; this is often accompanied by the feeling of warmth and acceptance;

this is the feeling associated with love. This explains why we are close with and even feel love for family, close friends and sexual partners. We are free to be open with them because we can open up to them and let down our defenses. This is what the new baby, born into the world does. It accepts and loves unconditionally. When insecurities creep in and scars are inflicted on our ego, that's when the defense mechanism rises up and our shield protection is activated. The only time we will feel free enough to let down our shields is when we are with people who accept us unconditionally.

Our first needs when we made our entrance into the world are to be fed, cleaned and cuddled etc. we are unconditionally accepting of everything in our environment. Our baby selves will communicate openly and spontaneously. Some of our basic ways of communication as babies is mainly by crying – for us to be fed, bathed, cleaned etc. as we grow a little older, our system of communication changes somewhat because we have more things we need to talk about.

Imagine the shock we received when we realize as we got older that not everyone is interested in communicating openly and spontaneously with us as we have been doing. Parents and other adults generally don't listen to us. True that they play with us and do relaxing things with us but some of us found that parents are not really interested in what we have to say. When they do respond to us, it mostly doesn't make sense because we don't understand it. Literally, we have stumbled on a play ground where no one wants to play with us.

Children are wired to believe that everything that happens is their fault. That is the way the mind of a child works and we are not any different. This why many traumas go in childhood and no one notices and it goes ahead and mares the child for life. For every single bad thing that happened, the child will seek to take the blame on himself. Often you hear, "if I were a good girl my parents wouldn't have divorced." As children we learn the concept of self-blame. Self-blame will later cause deep scars and insecurity. Invariably we would become involved in self-justification and even question our self-worth.

Had our parents the foresight to tell us it wasn't our fault that they were very much to blame for all we see go wrong in the family. Had they told us they were insecure and egotistical, it would have been much easier for the child in us to understand and deal with. In time we would have come to appreciate them for being open and sincerely about their feelings. The only problem with our being as children was that something is wrong with us because things around us are falling apart before our eyes. For this reason, we would seek ways to prove - if only to ourselves

- that we are wrong about whom we are. We want to prove that there is nothing really wrong with us. We become insecure in our thinking. Once insecurity steps in, we begin to act out. Our acting out comes from questioning our self-worth. We begin to suspect that we are not really worth much in the grand scheme of things. Our insecurities are what we project to the outside world when we act out. To prove our self-worth we do many silly things like shoplifting, writing graffiti on a wall or even fight in a war. We do all these things to prove to ourselves that we are worth more than we project. This is the point at which anger sets in. through anger we try to defend ourselves from the challenges we feel.

At this point in our lives, parents would begin to do some damage control by teaching us right from wrong. These things constitute the blueprint which we would need to follow for success. Then comes the feeling that if we fail to live up to the expectations of our parents in following the blueprint already set out, then we would have failed woefully indeed. Our parents' blueprint would become tied with our feeling of self-worth. This is when the feeling of guilt sets in and we learn an all new emotion.

There are important facts that naturally lead us to neurosis. The extent of our neurosis is dependent on these combined forces. The first force was the amount of positive communication we encountered early in life. By this, I mean how much of self-blame we felt growing up. Our value system and how it restricts us is the second force that contributes to our split nature. Let's say for example that we have pretty bad experiences that we are saddened and angry about but then we are not restricted by our conscience. It then means we will not repress our feelings in their entirety. We may go do some things to relieve tension like sex, weight lifting and walking but we still retain our capacity to love. On the other hand, if our value system places so much restrictions on us – like one who is born into a highly strict and religious home – relieving stress and energy through sex and partying would seem highly inappropriate. This strict moral code would always accuse and assault our insecure ego. In the end we would have increased anger and end up without the capacity for unconditional love.

Mating and Fixations

Children are naturally inquisitive. They would want to explore and find out what tickles their fancy. As would be expected, adults would often frown on what they see as inappropriate forms of exploration. Interestingly, once children have been told something is wrong, they may become fixated on it even into adulthood. For instance, a little boy may be told it is wrong to put on his sister's girly clothes. Now, this little boy may never get this message out of his head. He will forever wonder how it will feel to put on girly clothes and all. If he goes ahead to carry out this experiment he will meet with censor from adults and be told his behavior is unacceptable. This memory will stay with this child for a long time. His mind will keep going back to the moment when he was rejected and told what he did is unacceptable. He will re-create it a thousand times in his mind and sometimes act it out such that his behavior becomes acceptable. What we have is a boy that will seek to relive his fantasies by becoming a transvestite. He will be most comfortable in a community of transvestites who will accept him even though deep down his mind doesn't accept what he is doing.

A genuine problem arises when this fixation is on something dangerous and destructive. This may carry with it social taboo that is far beyond intolerance. This is exactly what happens with pedophilia. A child will normally become attracted to other children but once this attraction becomes a fixation, it may be carried into adulthood where it becomes a problem. This is even more serious if these feelings are acted upon and would cause serious harm to children. Even with the present situation, I will be quick to argue that the past cannot be undone and mere thoughts and emotions are morally neutral. But a pedophilic individual could not simply over look his actions and judge them to be comparable to the transvestite. Here he cannot say that his actions are harmless.

The good news for most of us is that we are quick to accept that which we are fixated about and move on with our lives. The same is the case with our sexuality. We accept that we are either attracted to people of the same gender and move on.

Sexuality is nothing to be ashamed about. Sexuality is much more than sex. Through mating we experience sexuality and that part of us that has always been there from birth. We will go through many stages in our life time about how we see our sexuality; like how we see our bodies, our emotions and values. Our sexuality helps us determine who we mate with, the gender we prefer as well as the kind of people that we prefer. It helps us to determine the values we appreciate and when, where and with whom this aspect of ourselves will be expressed.

Imagery

Human beings are imbued with the power of reason and imagination. Our ability to reason means that we gather and apply information to our situations and through logic and draw conclusions. However, when we use our imagination, we are giving our minds free reign without it being fettered by reality outside of itself.

Our ability to use our imagination serves some purposes one of which is the use of intuitions. Through reoccurrences in that exist in our universe we are able to use our imagination to observe similar patterns and perhaps learn from it. Storytellers use this imaginative function to their fullest advantage to weave stories and hold their audiences spellbound. While most of the stories that we have today may have been imagined but they are drawn from patterns in which the imaginations of the storytellers used experiences of real people to fashion their stories and seek understanding of the human nature. However, what we know as imagination is inexorably prophetic. This is why when we dream we are giving free reign to our imagination and as such we receive interpretations which are fulfilling. It follows that through the use of our imaginations we explore self. There are things that are missing in our lives that imagination can help us to fill; voids that would remain open unless we compensate for it through our imaginations. It is common for us to fantasize about things we couldn't have. We can imagine ourselves to be The Rock because we feel helpless and powerless. Our imagination can also provide an avenue for healing. Through our imagination we bring the separate parts of us to accept each other and become whole. We reconcile the different parts of us with each other.

The Power of Creative Imagery

In as much as we use creative imagery to our advantage but it can also draw us in and provide ideas that would scare the hell out of us. With our shield protection on – which represents our repressed state – it is easy for us to put our feelings in check but in the moments when our imaginations runs away with us, we find ourselves thinking deeply about those repressed sexual fantasies and thus we veer off the safe and narrow path. It is common for us to be angry about things we cannot change. We express our feelings of frustration through different ways. Our frustrations may be as a result of unmet sexual desires. In order not to feel out of place we only engage in sexual feeling which are considered appropriate and so those inappropriate feelings are suppressed and put in check. When we find ourselves thinking thoughts we feel are unwholesome, monstrous and depraved, it does not mean we are bad and monstrous. Our thoughts remind us of the things we are not. If we are as atrocious as we think we are because of our thoughts, then we would have acted on our thoughts long ago. But the fact that we did not means we are in a right place and will constantly remind ourselves of what we are not.

The thing about repressed feelings is that they could turn into something more serious. Restraining yourself from slapping someone if done repeatedly may turn our minds into imagining and even fantasizing about taking guns and committing mass murder. Anger and sexuality that is suppressed may lead to sexual fantasies that extreme and violent.

When we realize and accept that atrocious thoughts are nothing more than thoughts unless acted upon, we will understand that thoughts can't hurt anyone and we have to make the decision to change our thoughts to that which is good. Having a touch of humor never hurts; it can help us get over difficult situations.   . . . .

Living, the Way it is

One is can be described as being alive when there is free interaction of materials, energy and information in his body. When blood flows through the vein the way it is supposed to, there will be a proper passage of oxygen, nutrients and exchange of materials within the body. A living body can be at the peak of health when nothing impedes the free flow of information and the body systems responds efficiently to the needs of its immediate environment. The human body is a collection of cells all working in tandem with one another to ensure the smooth running of activities within the body. When sickness strikes, it doesn't stop the body from being alive. The rate and extent of bodily efficiency is what changes but it doesn't stop that body from living unless it is dead.

Our emotional and intellectual selves are alive in varying degrees. The degree to which we may be considered alive in this sense depends on our shield protection. When our emotions and intellectual ability is shield protected, free flow of information and emotion is closed off. The mind's ability to think clearly and logically is shut down and the result is the inability of the mind to see past its present set of emotion and ideas. A mind that is shielded is being prevented from enjoying the simple pleasures of life. Bodily sensations and expression of sensory pleasure becomes a thing of the past.

With the shield firmly in place, it will be difficult for us to interact freely with our immediate environment. In order to keep this shield firmly in place, we require a lot of energy and concentration. This makes it impossible to acknowledge the existence of factors outside of ourselves. Our character and body shields prevents us from reaching our full brain capacity. Ever wondered why most of us are only able to use about 10% of our brain capacity? It is because we have so shielded our character that we do not allow room for growth and development. Our complex shielded ego is why we look for other ways to function without having to face truths about ourselves.

In essence an individual with powerful defense mechanism such as the shield protection is not less alive than one who is very much without any form of protection. If being alive means freedom of thought, the ability of our sensory organs to feel and experience awareness, then both the shielded and non-shielded individual are alive but whether both are well is another story altogether.

We will take a clue from the teachings of Jesus while he was on earth in which he talked about life and death. Jesus talked about not having to die after death. What we draw from his inspirational discourse is that he may not be talking about physical death after all. Rather living an existence where one's shield protection is in full gear is a form of death where one is still living. Notice the emphasis he placed on sin which translates to selfishness and of course the solution to sin which is forgiveness – which in this sense is acceptance; which brings us to the conclusion that the key solution to living a shielded existence is through self-acceptance.

Then Comes the Scary Monster: Depression

Depression is a state of the mind in which the mood is low with an attendant aversion to activity. This can affect the thoughts, behavior sense of wellbeing and feelings of an individual. If we are depressed, we are angry, sad, anxious, empty, hopeless, helpless, worried, guilty, hurt, restless, and irritable. Activities that once interested us will lose their attraction. Concentration, remembering the details and decision making will present serious problems. Most times, depression is accompanied with insomnia, fatigue, pains, aches, digestive problems and suicidal feelings.

Let me make it clear that depression is not always a psychiatric disorder. It may take place as a result of normal life event, medical conditions or as a side effect of certain drugs. There are major kinds of depression. These are reactive and endogenous depression. In reactive depression, the trigger is usually an outside event such as death in the family, childbirth and a breakup in relationship. In the case of exogenous depression, there is no outside trigger; it appears spontaneously and takes hold.

As bad as depression sounds, it is always lurking in the shadows. When it strikes there is the feeling of worthlessness. The most common feeling amongst depressed people is self-hate. The four most common words to describe the feelings that follow are: defeated, defective, deserted and deprived. In your depressive state you begin to see yourself as being lacking in qualities that you value most in life. Your consciousness will allow free reign to negative feelings thus contributing hugely to a feeling of low self-esteem.

Rising out of your depressive state is important to your wellbeing. The best way to forge ahead is through an increase in the feeling of self-worth. Seeking to raise your self-esteem through your personal achievements is only temporary; it is simply pseudo-esteem. The first step is to understand the issues that resulted in your feeling of low self-esteem and then address it squarely.

Getting back to your feet is important and this will mean boosting your self-esteem. Often you hear that voice inside of you that says you are not worth it. There is often an internal critique inside of you. Traitorous thoughts of Inferiority complex, helplessness and self-doubt can be quenched by recognizing these thoughts for what they are. Write down these thoughts as they occur to you and learn why your thoughts are being distorted. Talk back to yourself and assert your authority. Counter your thoughts by saying you are none of the things your mind tells you. This helps to develop self-esteem that is more realistic.

Monitoring your negative thoughts is called mental biofeedback. This system allows you to do something about the way you feel much more than wishing things were different. In mental biofeedback, you write down all your negative thought for set periods of time each day. As you write, your mind will come up with more colorful and apt descriptions for your tarnished image. Do not hold back; write down things as they occur to you. Within 3 weeks, there is a strong probability that you will reach a plateau and all the negative thoughts will begin to go down. There will be far fewer things to write about. This indicates that you are beginning to accept yourself and all the harmful thoughts are diminishing.

Moping about your problems will reduce your ability to cope with it. Viewing your image in a moralistic and judgmental way will not only cloud your senses, it will also create confusion and despair. Your ability to deal with the problem at hand will be impeded and you can't get to the root of your problems. Getting rid of negative emotions and thoughts will make self-acceptance more feasible and your ability to cope will be enhanced.

Acceptance: it all Begins with Me

There is no royal road to self-acceptance. Beating yourself up at every opportunity will not solve the problem of acceptance. In fact, it is neurotic to look at your imperfections and berate yourself over and over again. Doing this is counterproductive as it will impede your chances for progress. You will find that your life and everything in it will improve remarkably if you practice self-acceptance. To experience a high level of self-esteem that we all want, you will have to self-accept yourself the way you are. This involves appreciating every facet of your personality; both the positive and so called negative attributes. If you will accept yourself you will need to forgive yourself. Take a break from your self-criticism and smell the roses in you.

Many of the challenges we experience in life come as a result of lack of self-esteem. It is no wonder that our relationships are subsequently affected. If you lack self-acceptance, there will be a tendency to hide the good attributes you have and mask it with something that is altogether not you. Soon, it will become apparent that you are only pretending to be what you are not. If lack of self-acceptance is allowed to linger, it will become a vicious cycle that destroys from within. With self-esteem at its lowest, it is easy to perceive that you are not liked by people when actually the reverse may be the case. The problem is not that you are not liked per say but the root of the whole matter is that people do not really know who you are to make informed decisions about you. If you can shed the mask for a moment and be yourself for once, you will find that people will be at ease in your presence and very much appreciate your company.

One thing about low self-esteem is that it causes you to be the under achiever. There is nothing you can do to propel yourself to your desired target. There is a marked lack of confidence that will enable you strive for success. No matter what you do, with a low self-esteem you will simply give up along the way in pushing for greater heights.

Rising from the low ebbs of self-esteem is achievable; what you need to do is to learn to forgive and accept yourself. Human beings will always make mistakes; it is the unwritten order of things amongst humans. You not only forgive yourself when things are not as palatable as you would wish. You forgive yourself, if you have done that which you feel is abominable. It doesn't end there. You also need to forgive others; including friends, family and relatives. We love our friends and family because they are imperfect and that's also one reason to forgive them for not being as perfect as you would have wished.

Every mistake that you have ever made in life should serve as a lesson moment for you. Unless what you have done has irrevocably hurt someone, then it is not really a mistake. If your life is full of lessons, then you will live a richer and rewarding life for it. It is sometimes inevitable that you will hurt the people you love in the process of making mistakes. This is just as well because it is the people that we love that will forgive us in a heartbeat. Don't wait to make amends later. Do so now and move on with your life. You owe it to yourself to succeed.

It is entirely possible that you actually like yourself as a person. You may be known as kind hearted by those who know you and they will go the extra mile for you. If you are like this, it is very much possible that your lack of self-acceptance has to do with your physical appearance. While the square jaw may look nice and strong but you would rather it were a little more sexy on you. There are a host of things to berate yourself about. Honestly, most people looking at you are not even thinking about your physical imperfections. The truth is that they don't care. Just like others are also caught up with their personal looks that there is simply no time to spare about your lack of pert nose. In all honesty, there is no such thing as an ugly man or woman. What one may find appealing in a person may be appalling to the next man. It is our different looks and sizes that makes interesting specimen. If you can give yourself some space and realize this, you will learn to view yourself the way you should; as a person with worth and interesting possibilities.

Your most important critic is yourself. You are the reason why you find it difficult accepting yourself the way you should. Understanding this about yourself is the most important step forward. The trick is to see yourself as others see you. Feel free to destroy your old image about yourself and start off with a new one. Decide to be fair and good to yourself. . . . .

The Wounds that fester

Even after many months and years have passed, we still find ourselves being hurt by past events. Each time we think of it our blood runs hot and we are filled with anger. What we suffer from is an emotional wound. Unlike physical wounds, emotional wounds can rarely be seen with the eyes and they do not heal quite as easily. The only similarity between physical and emotion wounds is that just like physical wounds, emotional wounds would form mental scar tissues to minimize and protect us from pain. This way we are able to move on with our lives.

With emotional pain we feel helpless and hopeless. There will be anger, resentment, lack of trust and even no trust at all. With the loss of self-esteem, it is easy to lose our confidence and passion. In feeling emotionally pained we are allowing our fears to take over and control us. With our fear of being rejected and abandoned in place, it is easy to be like the rolling stone that gathers no moss. We do the same things that we are afraid others would do to us.

Relationships are destroyed and love extinguished this way.

The key to healing from emotional wounds is by exploring and recognizing the scars. It is difficult to do but entirely achievable. It is easy to put your shield protection in place and pretend as if nothing happened but the truth is that the wound would ever remain beneath the surface. When a similar situation reoccurs, the wounds will resurface to cause great pain. When you recognize the enemy from within you and deal with it, you will begin the process of healing and development.

Now that the causes of the emotional wounds are glaring you in the face, it is time to find out what the root causes are. There must be a reason why you are hurt and angry. Look within yourself and find that moment when you snapped and became angry and hurt. That incident that affected you badly is what you need to concentrate on.

What is it about that situation that scared and hurt you the most?

In all that we do the past still firmly remains entrenched in the past. Neither you nor I can change our past. Your best bet is to accept your emotions and all that happened in the past. If you want to break loose from your past and emotional pains, then you don't need to fight them; just accept them.

The Child in Us

There is a child inside every one of us that wished things were different. Let me make it clear that the real child is more susceptible than the inner child in us. While the real child can easily get hurt and destroyed but the inner child remains unmoved through it all. The inner child cannot be killed or injured. The inner child in us represents our original nature; the nature that we were born with. The inner child serves to bring us unconditional love. Because of this inner child, it is very much possible for us to feel love without attaching any condition to it.

In a neurotic state, it is easy to get events and situations distorted. We may feel our inner child will judge us harshly for the things that we do. This way we wrongly assume that the inner child is the origin of our feeling of rejection, guilt and lack of self-acceptance. The inner child when viewed with mud tinted glasses will be seen as something evil. This is one of the major reasons why some people are hostile towards children for no apparent reason. This fear has created warped individuals who torture, molest and kill children because of this belief system.

One thing that escapes the tortured imagination is that the inner child can never condemn you. What it feels instead is unconditional love which is non-judgmental. This is why the Christian religion would call this inner child "God". God in the sense that we are sinful but God loves us still irrespective of our imperfections. Self-acceptance will reconnect us back with our inner child and eventually make us feel much better. It is the reunion that will bring us paradise. . . . .

A State of Awareness

A common misconception is the notion that self-esteem can be attained without self-judgment. When you estimate something, you are trying to appraise and judge. We judge ourselves against a certain standard without which we would seem to have failed ourselves. We see that self-esteem apparently comes with conditions. Through our prism we try to judge ourselves and see if we are living up to expectations. When we find ourselves wanting in a respect that is when we become fragmented and cut into pieces.

When we place self-esteem side by side with self-acceptance, one thing is apparent; it is that self-acceptance is unconditional. With self-acceptance you agree with yourself that you are the way you are and you will only do your best at each given moment. In the case of self-esteem, we evaluate against a given standard. We compare ourselves with others but when we come to accept the reality of who we are at each given moment that is when we have accepted ourselves. It will be right to say that whereas self-esteem is subjective, self-acceptance is free from evaluations and is therefore free from errors.

One of the things about self-acceptance is that it doesn't paralyze, instead it frees us up. With self-acceptance there is no mirror of comparisons and approval seeking. Clinging to praise and reliance on another's acceptance of you doesn't count with self-acceptance. A mind that is self-accepting will go about its normal business without caring what others think of him; he focuses on what's important and is immune to disapprovals. A self-accepting mind knows who he is and knows that other's opinion of him doesn't change anything about him. It is this perfect state that makes one to become self-aware.

Self-acceptance is the key to enjoying fulfilling, happy and healthy relationships. It is unfortunate that many people are not so accepting of themselves and as such relationships and people suffer as a result. It is easy to get immersed in old habits and not even be aware that something is wrong somewhere. It is only by creating a state of awareness that you can change patterns for the better. To create self-awareness, you must learn to accept yourself. This is the only way to move forward. To increase self-awareness, you must treat yourself with compassion. This is where the notion of compassionate self-awareness comes in. You are who you are; there is no doubts about that; accept it and move and at the same time show much empathy towards yourself.

When you increase self-awareness, you are willing to come to terms with your emotions and understand yourself from your own perspective. You need to come to terms with your struggles with the desire to heal from your pains. Rather than attacking yourself incessantly, why not show yourself some sympathy instead? There are several roads to compassionate self-awareness but they all involve paying close attention to yourself, become aware of your bitterness and other negative feelings. Don't carry the burden all alone; share with a supportive friend and keep a journal of your thoughts and journey.

It is difficult to be aware and open up old and fresh wounds about yourself. One of the sure ways that will make the process easier is through meditation and mindfulness. How do you treat yourself? Do you see yourself as someone that deserves compassion and respect? Are you a friend to yourself? These questions will help you start the process of self-awareness. Another way that works is by being compassionate to others first instead of yourself. Treat your family, friends, colleagues and strangers with respect. Then, apply the same attitude to yourself. The reason for this is that if you don't know how to treat yourself with compassion and respect, you can learn how to do so by doing it to others. Only then can you apply the principle that worked for you with others to yourself. Self-awareness can be reassuring and help you nurture a sense of wellbeing with your environment.

Many people automatically assume that they are self-aware without weighing themselves in the emotional scale. Self-awareness has nothing to do with bits and pieces of information about yourself. It has to do with your ability to see the larger picture about yourself and at the same time be conscious enough to acknowledge the small fine details that will otherwise elude you. Minute details about your emotions and self are usually where the larger picture lies. If you can piece them together, you will form a large picture and know where you are headed with your life.

Creating self-awareness is important
Developing self-awareness is an important step in the right direction. There will be noticeable changes in thoughts and interpretations as events play across your mind. When your interpretation is changed, your emotions are

redirected and changed likewise. In order to achieve success, self-awareness must take place and this will lead to emotional intelligence.

Self-mastery is all achievable through the process of self-awareness. Projecting what you want will make you focus your mind and attention to it. Invariably, the direction of your emotions, reactions, personality and behavior will determine your path in life.

When you are aware, you are conscious of the direction of your thoughts and emotions and as such you can have a firmer control over them. Unless you are self-aware, you will never have control over your behavior, thoughts, words and emotions. Making changes to your life will become increasingly difficult as a result.

Developing self-awareness requires constant practice. It may not happen overnight but it is possible. Self-awareness cannot simply be learned by reading, you need to practice to become good at it. Think of self-awareness as learning how to dance. When we dance, we pay close attention to the movement of our feet, the beats, motion and floor space, other dancers and the way our body sways to the music. You need to pay close attention before you can get it right.

When you finally become self-aware you begin to see snippets of your personality that you were not altogether aware of. You will begin to see things that need to change about you. Small things or events that serve as triggers to your emotional trauma will immediately become apparent. You will notice the moment when your mind begins to interpret events differently. In this heightened state of awareness, you will instinctively know to make better and wise choices. The process will begin unconsciously in your mind and change your outlook and perception before destructive emotional reaction will set in.

The Kingdom Suffereth Violence

It is no mean feat to acknowledge the truth about you. It can be a painful process if you don't know how to start and how to control your feelings. Our basic nature is meant to be healthy and it actually is. The problem is that the ways we choose to tackle our problems is totally not helpful given the harsh way we look at ourselves. Immediately we grab a hold of the truth about us, we are free indeed.

The result of the chink in our shield is anger. In our anger we feel someone is trying to gain unlawful entrance into our privacy; that place we hold sacred. As a result, we have no options than to fire mercilessly at the intruder. This is the way anger functions. Truth be told, we indeed have options about how we react to situations. Anger in itself is not entirely bad. It is a part of our emotions that will enable us to be whole. When anger is expressed in a healthy way, we have a constructive tool in our hands but let it out of control and you have a weapon of mass destruction that will only leave sorrow and more anger in its wake.

Every individual has a belief system that he abides by. It is possible to determine whether this belief system is truthful by careful monitoring of this individual's behavior. Where a belief system is healthy and true, it will rhyme with reality and will require little effort on the part of the individual to maintain. Compare this belief system to one that is fabricated, it is easy to see that great efforts and a good measure of discipline are required to keep the fabricated belief system afloat. With the fabricated belief system that is built on falsehood, you have to be on alert and on guard to block out any contrary evidence. If your defense mechanism is based on fabricated falsehood, there will be more cracks on your shield. This means you are likely to get angry all the time.

The pull of anger is a very strong one. Sometimes the pull may get so strong that we may not freely express our anger in words and pass our message across. This is when violence comes into the equation. Violence is the language when words become too cumbersome. This is when the truth finally dawns on us; that our violent behavior totally invalidates our belief system, leaving it bare for all to see what it is. Violence tells us that our belief system is faulty, fabricated and built on falsehood.

Feeding the violent with violence will serve no purpose at all. Don't allow violent people to drain your energy. It is understandable if we are stepping in to stop them from hurting people but the only way that change will come to the violent is by allowing them to witness the collapse that comes from their violent nature.

Hope on the Horizon

Our original nature is one characterized by love unconditional. This unconditional love can be set free when we are confident in ourselves to be able to drop our shields. What humans lack is unconditional love of self. The more we riddle ourselves with dogmas and other social burdens we are building on our shield. A sudden breakdown in our shield protection can be painful and may even be destructive. It is far more preferable if there is a gradual erosion of the shield by deep understanding of our place in life.

We may not have control over what takes place all around us but we can decide to take the positive side of life and see things change for good. When we realize that our belief system is faulty and erroneous, we will be able to face the truth about ourselves. We will be more open to new ideas and perhaps touch people who otherwise would be inaccessible to us. There is the need for the old neurotic world as we know it to die so that the birth of a new world will take place.

www.ingramcontent.com/pod-product-compliance
Lightning Source LLC
Chambersburg PA
CBHW042340150426
43196CB00001B/7